FEDERAL
HABEAS CORPUS

FEDERAL HABEAS CORPUS

PRACTICE COMMENTARIES
AND STATUTES

STEVEN M. STATSINGER

NATIONAL INSTITUTE FOR TRIAL ADVOCACY

Statsinger, Steven M., *Federal Habeas Corpus Commentaries and Statutes* (NITA, 2002)

ISBN 1-55681-804-1

8/02

CONTENTS

▮▮▮

Title 28, Chapter 154. §§ 2261-2266

PREFACE

■■■

The writ of habeas corpus has long been a means of protecting individuals against the tyranny of the state. But the writ is far from a historical relic, and the need for its protection is as great today as it ever has been.

One need only pick up a newspaper to see why. Hardly a week goes by without a new report of some troubling and unprecedented form of government action. Whether it be prisoners detained seemingly indefinitely at Guantanamo Bay or American citizens jailed without charges and denied access to counsel, it is readily apparent that the writ of habeas corpus continues to provide a remedy that is critical to maintaining a fair and just society.

And it is not just the war on terrorism that has prompted this observation. Another all-too common occurrence recently has been the revelation that a prisoner condemned to die or one serving an unusually long non-capital sentence, has been exonerated and released. A survey of some of the shocking statistics in this area can be found in Judge Jed. S. Rakoff's courageous opinion in *United States v. Quinones*, 196 F.Supp.2d 416 (S.D.N.Y. 2002).

Attorneys have a special obligation to help right such wrongs. As of this writing there are literally hundreds of prisoners under a sentence of death whose claims have gone unheard because they lack counsel. Pro bono opportunities abound, however, to provide assistance to this sorely underrepresented group. The commentaries that follow are intended to serve as a primer to those who are uninitiated into the intricacies of habeas corpus practice. Any reader of these materials who uses them to lend assistance to someone who is without funds, but in need of counsel, will not only learn firsthand how satisfying pro bono work can be, but will also earn the admiration and gratitude of their author.

Steven M. Statsinger
July 2002

INTRODUCTION

∎∎∎

Federal Habeas Corpus Commentaries and Statutes

These commentaries offer a brief, practical discussion of the habeas corpus process, written from the viewpoint of the author, Steven Statsinger, a federal public defender. Those new to environments where habeas corpus is used, will find that the commentaries provide a quick, clear description of the process. Those experienced in these proceedings will find commentaries a useful summation with what we hope will be new, practical advice. The statutes relating to habeas corpus are included in the second part of this book for quick reference.

The writ of habeas corpus has a long and noble tradition in English law. With vestiges in the Magna Carta, a writ of habeas corpus was used with varying degree of success to thwart the king's arbitrary seizure and detention of his subjects from the twilight of common law to the Seventeenth Century. In 1679, in response to the king's increasingly effective circumvention of the writ, the English Parliament passed the Habeas Corpus Act as "an act for the better securing the liberty of the subject, and for the prevention of imprisonments beyond the seas."

Habeas Corpus, "that you have the body," is a writ or order requiring a person having the custody of another to produce "that body" and the court would determine whether the detention was procedurally correct. A habeas corpus proceeding does not determine guilty or innocence, but often the issue of procedural correctness is wrapped up in substantive issues.

Use and abuse of the habeas corpus process was frequent in the American Colonial period, and according to some, the denial of the habeas corpus right to the colonials contributed to the discontent that led to the American Revolution. Habeas corpus proceedings are in state and federal constitutions, but there are cases where such protections have been suspended. Massachusetts did so in 1786 during Shay's Rebellion, as did Lincoln with Congress's approval during the Civil War.

Originally habeas corpus proceedings were intended for those imprisoned, but modern usage in the United States includes divorce and adoption cases where the custody of children is at issue.

The National Institute for Trial Advocacy (NITA) plans to publish several companion pamphlets that explore topics including surveillance and constitutional issues. Visit the NITA Web site at www.nita.org or call (800) 225-6482 for more information.

Frank Alan
Electronic Publishing Editor
National Institute for Trial Advocacy

Overview *title*
28 USCS §§ 2241-2255

a para rule

Purpose *para title*

(a) and body

The purpose of a habeas corpus petition is to seek an order from a federal court releasing a person who is in custody in violation of the United States Constitution. A habeas corpus proceeding is a separate civil proceeding that is entirely distinct from the criminal trial and its direct appeals. For this reason, it is known as a "collateral" or "post-conviction" proceeding.

Since a habeas corpus petition challenges the lawfulness of a prisoner's custody, the party sued is generally the person responsible for the custody, such as the administrator of the facility where the person is incarcerated, or the commissioner of corrections in that jurisdiction. Most states, by statute, provide for an intrastate, post-conviction collateral review process. A federal court's authority to provide collateral relief derives from 28 USCS § 2241(a), which authorizes federal judges to grant writs of habeas corpus. However, only prisoners who meet one of the five criteria set out in § 2241(c) are eligible for federal habeas corpus relief.

Most applications for federal habeas corpus relief are filed under 28 USCS § 2254, which authorizes a prisoner in custody pursuant to a judgment of a state court to seek federal court review. Prisoners in custody under a federal sentence may seek an equivalent form of relief by moving to vacate the sentence under section 2255. In a small number of additional cases where the prisoner or claim does not fit neatly in either of these categories, the prisoner can file an application for relief under section 2241. Regardless of the statute invoked, the procedures that apply, and the significant hurdles that the applicant faces, are similar.

Practice under the habeas corpus statutes is among the most complex areas of federal litigation. It is governed not just by statute, but by the Federal Rules of Civil Procedure, two sets of procedural rules promulgated solely for habeas corpus petitions, various courts' local rules, and a significant body of case law not codified in any statute or rule. Moreover, since the petition itself will always contain allegations of constitutional violations that occurred during a criminal proceeding or in connection with some other aspect of the custody, significant expertise in constitutional law and criminal law and procedure is also required. Further complicating matters is the general preference in federal habeas corpus jurisprudence for giving states the first opportunity to resolve the federal issues. In many cases this will necessitate a return to state court to present an issue through the state's own post-conviction review process, another complex area of practice that will have to be mastered.

These complexities are rendered all the more daunting by virtue of the fact that most prisoners who seek habeas corpus relief are not entitled to court-appointed counsel, and end up proceeding *pro se*. Sections 2254 and 2255 permit, but do not require, the appointment of counsel on request of the prisoner seeking relief. Indigent prisoners under sentence of death, however, are entitled to appointed counsel, along with investigative, expert and other reasonably necessary services to assist in the preparation of their application. 21 USCS § 848(q)(4)(B).

Scope of the practice commentaries

The habeas corpus statutes were radically amended, effective April 24, 1996, by the Anti-Terrorism and Effective Death Penalty Act (AEDPA). Although there is a large body of pre-AEDPA law, virtually all newly filed petitions are governed by AEDPA. Thus, these commentaries are geared primarily to AEDPA practice.

Many of the statutes in Chapter 153 are directions to the court, not the practitioner, and require little explanation here. For example, section 2243 discusses largely housekeeping matters. Similarly, sections 2245, 2246, 2247, 2248, 2249, 2250, and 2252 are self-explanatory, giving clear instructions about certain procedural matters. Except for a few passing references, they are not discussed in these commentaries.

These commentaries are intended primarily to provide guidance in practice under section 2254, but be will also be suitable for applications filed under the sections 2254 and 2241. They are organized around the sequence of events that normally take place in any habeas corpus proceeding. The first commentary discusses the form, content, and timing of an application for habeas corpus relief, as well as stays. This is followed by individual commentaries about the three sections under which federal relief is available: 28 USCS § 2254, 28 USCS § 2255, and 28 USCS § 2241. The series ends with commentaries relating to evidentiary hearings and discovery, relief and appeals, and second or subsequent applications.

The statutes in Chapter 153 generally refer to the prisoner as the "applicant," and to the filing as the "application." Practitioners tend call the prisoner the "petitioner" and the filing a "petition" if it is filed under §§ 2254 or 2241 or a "motion" if it is filed under § 2255. In these commentaries the two sets of terms are used interchangeably.

Form, Content, Timing, and Stays
28 USCS § 2242

[handwritten annotations: Title Common v.d. / ITC Common 14 pt / (a) and body]

According to 28 USCS § 2242 and the rules governing habeas corpus petitions, an application for a writ of habeas corpus must be legibly handwritten or typed and must be "signed and verified by the person for whose relief it is intended or by someone acting in his behalf." A verification is a statement that the application is signed under penalty of perjury.

If filed under 28 USCS § 2254, the petition must include a form similar to that annexed to the federal habeas corpus rules. There are separate rules for motions under 28 USCS § 2255 and also a different model form. The clerk's office in the district court should have a form available that meets the local rules. The application form should be accompanied by either the appropriate filing fee or an affidavit of indigence plus a request for poor person's status, a motion for appointment of counsel if the prisoner is indigent, and an application for a stay of execution in capital cases. Those motions that are necessary for fact development in the case, such as requests for an evidentiary hearing or discovery, can be filed with the application or can be filed later, subject to the schedule set by the court. Two conformed copies should accompany the original petition.

The form petition provides relatively little space for legal argument, so it is generally a good idea to prepare a separate memorandum of law. This can be filed along with the petition or later, subject to the schedule set by the court. The brief should support all of the legal arguments contained in the petition, both factually and legally, and should also oppose any defenses raised by the state.

28 USCS § 2242 sets out the only statutory requirement for the content of the habeas corpus application: the application must contain "the facts concerning the applicant's commitment or detention, the name of the person who has custody over him and by

virtue of what claim or authority, if known." In practice, the petition should contain a description of the prisoner's custody status, including the current sentence he is serving, the judgments and convictions under which petitioner is detained, a statement describing the manner by which the claims have been exhausted, a description of any other federal habeas corpus petitions filed by the petitioner along with an explanation of why the present claims were not made earlier, the legal and factual claims for the assertion that the custody is unlawful, and a prayer for relief.

Before deciding which claims to include in a petition, the habeas practitioner must carefully evaluate the record of the prior proceedings, consult the client and former counsel, and reinvestigate any important factual issues. Under the Anti-Terrorism and Effective Death Penalty Act (AEDPA) a prisoner will generally have an opportunity to file only one application; therefore the petition should include all colorable grounds for relief. This is true even if some of the claims are not well developed factually at the time of filing, since additional fact development is often permitted.

There is a tension between this advice and the requirement that petitions containing both exhausted and unexhausted claims be dismissed. Nevertheless, since there are often ways to exhaust unexhausted claims after the application has been filed, they should probably be included.

Just about any type of constitutional violation can be the subject of a habeas corpus petition. Constitutional error can infect every stage of the criminal proceeding, from investigation and accusation, through trial, sentencing, and appeal. However, the Fourth Amendment presents a significant exception to the habeas applicant's ability to raise constitutional error. Where the petitioner had a full and fair opportunity to litigate a Fourth Amendment claim in the state court, and was represented by competent counsel, he is barred from pursuing that claim in a collateral proceeding. *Stone v. Powell*, 428 U.S. 465, 49 L.Ed.2d 1067, 96 S.Ct. 3037 (1976).

A comprehensive list of the kinds of issues that might result in habeas corpus relief is beyond the scope of this commentary. But a helpful, if non-exhaustive, framework is to follow the course of a criminal case through its various stages. At the investigation stage, habeas corpus relief could be sought based on constitutional defects in securing a confession or in a pretrial identification process. At the accusation stage, claims might be based on defects in the charging instrument that result in a lack of fair notice, improper joinder of counts or defendants, or double jeopardy violations. Discovery-related claims would include the suppression of exculpatory evidence. Constitutional defects in the jury selection process or the exposure of the jury to prejudicial pretrial publicity might warrant relief. The number and types of error that could occur at trial would include evidentiary rulings that violate a constitutional right, prosecutorial misconduct, violations of the defendant's right to be present or to a public trial, or erroneous jury instructions. A claim that the conviction was based on legally insufficient evidence can be raised in a habeas corpus petition, as can a host of issues relating to sentencing, particularly in capital cases. And finally, a claim that counsel was constitutionally ineffective at <u>any</u> stage of the proceedings, up to and including the direct appeal, is also cognizable in a habeas corpus petition.

Timing of applications

Perhaps the most significant procedural barrier raised by AEDPA is the one-year statute of limitations, which is jurisdictional. A habeas corpus petition must be filed within one year of the latest of four different dates: (1) the date on which the judgment became final by the conclusion of direct appellate review or the expiration of the time for seeking such review, (2) the date on which any impediment to filing the application created by illegal government action was removed, (3) the date on which any new constitutional right was recognized and made retroactively applicable to cases on collateral review by the Supreme Court, or (4) the date on which the facts supporting the claim could have been discovered through due diligence. 28 USCS §§ 2244(d), 2255. In almost all cases, however, only the first of these options will be relevant. Section 2244(d)(2) contains a tolling provision. The time during which a prisoner's properly filed petition for state court post-conviction relief is pending is excluded from the one-year limitations period.

Prisoners filing *pro se* petitions can comply with the statute of limitations by placing their petition in the prison mail system on or before the filing deadline.

Stays

28 USCS § 2251 authorizes the federal judge to stay any state proceeding against the petitioner, as long as the petition for habeas corpus relief is pending before that judge. This procedure is utilized most frequently where the petitioner has been sentenced to death. In such cases, the application for a stay of execution should be filed along with the petition itself or as soon as practicable afterwards. When an indigent prisoner under sentence of death applies to the district court for appointment of counsel under 21 USCS § 848(q)(4)(B), the court should issue a stay of execution to ensure that counsel has adequate time to prepare the petition. McFarland v. Scott, 512 U.S. 849, 129 L.Ed.2d 666, 114 S.Ct. 2568 (1994).

Applications for Federal Relief 𝑇𝑖𝑡𝑙𝑒
28 USCS § 2255

Section 2254 sets out the basic requirements for a "person in custody pursuant to the judgment of a State court" to apply for federal relief based on a claim that he is in custody in violation of the constitution. The petition may be filed in the district court either in the district where the petitioner is incarcerated or the district where the petitioner was convicted. 28 USCS § 2241(d).

The custody requirement

The first requirement of § 2254 is that the defendant be "in custody," a term that is broader than imprisonment on the judgment of conviction. Any person who is "subject to restraints not shared by the public generally" is in custody. *Hensley v. Municipal Court*, 411 U.S. 345, 351, 36 L.Ed.2d 294, 300, 93 S.Ct. 1571, 1575 (1973). Custody therefore includes probation or parole, prison furloughs, serving a suspended or stayed sentence, a sentence requiring the payment of a fine together with a threat of incarceration to compel payment, or release pending the execution of sentence.

Even if a sentence is expired, a person can be in custody as a result of the sentence if its adverse collateral consequences are serious enough. The most common cases are those where the prisoner is serving another sentence that was enhanced by the sentence challenged. Also, where a prisoner is serving consecutive sentences, he is considered to be "in custody" on any one of them for the purposes of filing a petition under section 2254. *Peyton v. Rowe*, 391 U.S. 54, 67, 20 L.Ed.2d 426, 435, 88 S.Ct. 1556 (1968).

Exhaustion and procedural default

The second requirement of section 2254 is that the defendant must exhaust the remedies available in the state courts. 28 USCS § 2254(b)(1)(A). This rule requires the petitioner to first present his claims to all state courts empowered to act on such claims before seeking relief from the federal courts. Although section 2254(c) does not deem state remedies exhausted until "any available procedure" has been utilized to raise the issue in the state courts, this test is usually satisfied if the claim was pursued to the end of available direct appeals. In other words, in most instances a claim that was properly presented all the way through the state court's appellate process need not also be pursued through the state's post-conviction process to be deemed exhausted. On the other hand, those claims that were not pursued on direct appeal or that do not lend themselves to a direct appeal (such as claims of ineffective assistance of counsel based on facts not evident on the face of the record), must first be exhausted through the state court post-conviction process before they can be entertained in a federal petition.

Federal courts must dismiss petitions based entirely on un-exhausted claims or "mixed petitions" containing both exhausted and unexhausted claims. There are three dismissal options for unexhausted claims. The applicant should either request that the dismissal be without prejudice to reinstate the petition after he has exhausted the claims, or request that the petition be held in abeyance pending the return to state court. Either of these options will almost invariably require exhaustion through the state's post-conviction process. Alternatively, a mixed petition may be amended to merely abandon any unexhausted claims. The unexhausted claims could then be pursued in state court, but given the strict rules for filing second or successive federal habeas corpus petitions, it is unlikely that federal review would be available for those claims in the future.

Under 28 USCS § 2254(b)(1)(B), the exhaustion requirement is waived where there is an "absence of available State corrective process" or where circumstances exist that would render such process "ineffective to protect the rights of the applicant." Federal courts only rarely find that either of these tests has been met. The application of these tests to a particular case will turn on a detailed analysis of the applicable state court post-conviction process and the issues presented in the particular case. The exhaustion requirement can also be waived by the state in its response to the petition, but such waiver must be expressed. 28 USCS § 2254(b)(3). If it is clear that a claim is unexhausted, it is unlikely that the state will waive this defense unless the state believes that the claim is so entirely frivolous that judicial economy would best be served by denying it on the merits.

A failure to exhaust state remedies is not the only procedural hurdle facing a state prisoner. "Procedural default" is equally important, although it appears nowhere in the statute. Procedural default occurs where the petitioner has failed to raise his federal claim in the state court in the manner prescribed by state law. Such default often occurs when trial counsel did not satisfy a state's contemporaneous objection rule in some way, either by failing to object to an error, or by doing so without sufficient specificity or at the wrong time, and the state appellate courts have unambiguously denied the claim on this ground. Procedural default precludes federal relief because the claim has been decided on an adequate and independent state law ground. Procedural default must be asserted by the state as a defense; if the state does not assert procedural default, the defense is waived.

Procedural default is excusable if the petitioner satisfies a two-part standard known as the "cause and prejudice" test. *Coleman v. Thompson*, 501 U.S. 722, 115 L.Ed.2d 640, 111 S.Ct. 2546 (1991). "Cause" is some objective factor external to the defense that impeded trial counsel's efforts to comply with the state's procedural rule. It can be a positive impediment, such as a judge's refusal to let counsel to make an objection, or a negative impediment, such as the unavailability of the legal or factual predicate for the objection, or the ineffectiveness of counsel. "Prejudice" generally means that the claimed constitutional error worked to the petitioner's actual and substantial disadvantage. The Supreme Court has not defined the prejudice prong any more precisely than this, but its nearest equivalent is the harmless error standard applicable in habeas corpus cases set out in *Brecht v. Abrahamson*, 507 U.S. 619, 123 L. Ed. 2d 353, 113 S. Ct. 1710, 1993 U.S. LEXIS 2981 under which an error must be shown to have had a "substantial and injurious effect or influence in determining the jury's verdict." The proponent of a "prejudice" argument will have to argue that the outcome of the proceeding would have been different but for the error.

A second exception to procedural default is the "miscarriage of justice" exception. Under this exception, a procedural default will be excused if the petitioner can demonstrate that the failure to consider the claims will result in a fundamental miscarriage of justice. *Coleman*, 501 U.S. at 722, 115 L.Ed.2d at 640, 111 S.Ct. at 2546. The Court has only conclusively applied this exception to claims of actual innocence, that is, where it can be shown that the constitutional violation "probably" resulted in the conviction of one actually innocent of the crime of conviction (*Murray v. Carrier*, 477 U.S. 478 L.E.2d S.Ct. (1986)) or of a death sentence. *Duger v. Adams*, 489 U.S. 401 L.E.2d S.Ct. (1989).

Both procedural default and lack of exhaustion can sometimes be avoided by asserting in the habeas corpus petition that trial counsel's failure to object to a constitutional violation, causing a procedural default, or to pursue it on appeal, causing an exhaustion problem, constituted ineffective assistance of counsel under the Sixth Amendment. Of course, the ineffective assistance claim would itself have to be first exhausted, usually through the state court's own collateral review process. Under 28 USCS § 2254(i), however, ineffectiveness of counsel in either a state or a federal post-conviction proceeding cannot itself be the basis for federal habeas relief.

Standards of review

In additional to procedural bars, state prisoners face significant substantive hurdles before federal relief can be granted. If a claim has survived all of the various procedural pitfalls, the federal court will review it on the merits under a standard that is extremely deferential to the state court's legal and factual determinations.

A petition cannot be granted with respect to any legal claim unless the state court's adjudication of that claim "resulted in a decision that was contrary to, or involved an unreasonable application of, clearly established Federal law as determined by the Supreme Court of the United States." 28 USCS § 2254(d)(1). A decision is "contrary to" Supreme Court precedent where "the state court arrives at a conclusion opposite to that reached by [the Supreme Court] on a question of law or if the state court decides a case differently than th[e] Court has on a set of materially indistinguishable facts." *Williams v. Taylor*, 529 U.S. 362, 146 L.Ed.2d 389, 120 S.Ct. 1495 (2000).

An "unreasonable application" of the Court's precedent occurs where the state court's decision was objectively unreasonable, meaning that the state court "identifie[d] the correct governing legal principle from th[e] Court's decisions but unreasonably applie[d] that principle to the facts of the prisoner's case." *Id.* "Unreasonable" is not synonymous with "incorrect," thus an incorrect application of Supreme Court precedent will only trigger federal relief if it is also unreasonable. One case that illustrates this distinction is *Neal v. Puckett*, 239 F.3d 683, 693-97 (5th Cir. 2001). There, the court considered a claim that defense counsel had been ineffective in not presenting readily available mitigating information at a capital sentencing. The court found that the Mississippi Supreme Court had incorrectly applied the prejudice prong of the *Strickland* standard, but nevertheless denied relief because it concluded that the state court had not unreasonably applied *Strickland*.

Section 2254(d)(1) also codifies, in somewhat stricter form, the non-retroactivity rule of *Teague v. Lane*, 489 U.S. 288, 103 L.Ed.2d 334, 109 S.Ct. 1060 (1989). Under *Teague*, a petitioner could not seek relief based on the retroactive application of a "new rule" of constitutional law if that rule was announced after his conviction became final. Section 2254(d)(1) tightens the *Teague* non-retroactivity rule, limiting relief to claims based on legal rules <u>actually in effect when the state court decided the case</u>, as opposed to those in effect during the much longer period that elapses before the conviction becomes final. Moreover, while *Teague* permitted the petitioner to rely on decisions of lower federal courts, § 2254(d)(1) limits review to claims based on Supreme Court decisions only. The *Teague* rule also bore some exceptions; these exceptions are not mentioned in the statute. While the Supreme Court has not extensively explored the relationship between *Teague* and cases governed by the stricter AEDPA provision, it is safe to say that those exceptions are no longer available.

There are equally challenging substantive barriers to claims based on state court factual error. Under § 2254(e)(1), state court factual determinations are presumptively correct, and the petitioner can rebut this presumption only by clear and convincing evidence. Moreover, § 2254(d)(2) prohibits relief unless the state court's factual determination was "unreasonable" in light of "the evidence presented in the State court proceeding." The Supreme Court has not yet construed this provision, although it is likely that a definition quite similar to that set out in *Williams* would apply. One case applying section 2254(d)(2) is *Mastracchio v. Vose*, 274 F.3d 590 (1st Cir. 2001), where the habeas corpus petition was based in part on a claim that the state had failed to disclose to the defense the special favors that a cooperating witness had received while in prison. The state courts had determined that various pretrial disclosures of a general nature had sufficiently apprised the defense, but the federal court concluded that this finding of fact was unreasonable given the large amount of detail that was only discovered after the trial. *Id.* at 598-99.

A federal prisoner alleging that he is in custody in violation of habeas corpus principles proceeds by filing a motion to vacate his sentence under 28 USCS § 2255. The motion must be filed in the district court where the prisoner was sentenced. Section 2255 provides four grounds for relief: (1) "the sentence was imposed in violation of the Constitution or laws of the United States;" (2) "the court was without jurisdiction to impose such sentence;" (3) "the sentence was in excess of the maximum authorized by law;" or, (4) "is otherwise subject to collateral attack." Despite this seemingly broad language, the Supreme Court has indicated that § 2255 relief should be granted only in cases where a "fundamental defect" caused a "complete miscarriage of judge." *Davis v. United States*, 417 U.S. 333, 345, 41 L.Ed.2d 109, 119, 94 S.Ct. 2298, 2305 (1974).

Applicants under section 2255 have essentially the same procedural hurdles—exhaustion and procedural default—to overcome as do state prisoners.

Federal prisoners are subject to a procedural default rule under which relief is barred if the issue was not properly noticed at trial. This can be excused under a cause and prejudice exception similar to that permitted under section 2254. *United States v. Frady*, 456 U.S. 152, 71 L.Ed.2d 819, 102 S.Ct. 1584 (1982). Similarly, although the statute does not contain an exhaustion requirement, most courts have held that, absent a showing of cause and prejudice a direct appeal is a necessary prerequisite to relief under this section. As is the case for petitions under § 2254, "cause" is some objective factor external to the defense that impeded counsel's efforts to comply with the state's procedural rule. It can be a positive impediment, such as a judge's refusal to let counsel to make an objection, or a negative impediment, such as the unavailability of the legal or factual predicate for the objection, or the ineffectiveness of counsel. "Prejudice" generally means that the claimed constitutional error worked to the petitioner's actual and substantial disadvantage.

In addition, a § 2255 motion will usually be dismissed if it raises claims that were previously decided on direct appeal, on the theory that there has already been adequate federal review of the claim.

These rules leave the petitioner in something of a quandary. He is barred from pursuing the issues that were raised on his direct appeal, but is also barred from raising those that were not, seemingly leaving him without any issues at all for the 2255 motion. In almost all cases, therefore, a § 2255 motion will be based on one or more of three types of claims: (1) an intervening change in the law; (2) a claim that counsel was ineffective that could not be raised on direct appeal because it is based on facts not apparent from the face of the record; or (3) a claim based on newly discovered evidence.

In a few rare instances a federal prisoner's custody will fall outside the categories contemplated by section 2255. In those instances, the prisoner may file a habeas corpus petition under 2241.

Indeed, section 2255 itself recognizes that a habeas corpus petition may be filed by a federal prisoner in those cases where a motion under § 2255 will be "inadequate or ineffective to test the legality" of the detention.

A section 2241 application is typically filed in cases involving: a federal prisoner's challenge to something other than his conviction or sentence, such as an action of the United States Parole Commission or the Federal Bureau of Prisons; a service member in custody seeking federal court review of a military conviction; or an alien detained by the Immigration and Naturalization Service. In these situations the prisoner must first exhaust all administrative or other available other remedies before filing the section 2241 petition.

The various procedural restrictions imposed by AEDPA do not apply to petitions under § 2241. *I.N.S. v. St. Cyr*, 522 U.S. 289, 150 L.Ed.2d 347,121 S.Ct. 2271 (2001). Most notably, several courts have held that a 2255 motion or a 2254 petition that follows a petition filed under 2241 is not a "second or successive" petition under AEDPA. *Jacobs v. McCaughtry*, 251 F.3d 596 (7th Cir. 2001)(*per curiam*); *Chambers v. United States*, 106 F.3d 472 (2d Cir. 1997).

Evidentiary Hearings and Discovery
28 USCS § 2246

The vast majority of habeas corpus applications are resolved based on the papers alone; after reviewing the documents, a judge will either decide the application based on the merits, or dismiss the application due to some sort of procedural default. If a case cannot be disposed of in this manner, an evidentiary hearing is necessary.

The right to a hearing in habeas corpus cases is governed principally by two Supreme Court Cases, *Townsend v. Sain*, 372 U.S. 293, 9 L.Ed.2d 770, 83 S.Ct. 745 (1963), *partially overruled by*, *Keeney v. Tamayo-Reyes*, 504 U.S. 1, 118 L.Ed.2d 318, 112 S.Ct. 1715 (1992). These cases require that a hearing be held where, through no fault of the applicant, the state court made no determination on a factual question, the state court's determination is not supported by the record, or the determination was made after an unfair procedure. Where the application alleges facts that, if proved, would entitle the petitioner to relief, a hearing should be granted, but is not required.

If there was no factual determination in the state court and the applicant was at fault for this, the case will be governed by 28 USCS § 2254(e)(2), an AEDPA addition. Under 28 USCS § 2254(e)(2) there can be no hearing unless the claim relies on a previously unavailable Supreme Court decision that is retroactive to cases on collateral review; or the applicant satisfies a stringent cause and prejudice standard. This restriction applies only where the applicant's failure to develop the factual claim in state court resulted from a lack of diligence; if efforts were made to develop the claim, but those efforts were unsuccessful, there has been no failure to develop the claim within the meaning of section 2254(e)(2). *Williams v. Taylor*, 529 U.S. 420, 146 L.Ed.2d 435, 120 S.Ct. 1479 (2000).

In preparation for an evidentiary hearing, the litigants are entitled to discovery under FRCP 26(a), including depositions and production of documents or other physical materials. Section 24 permits oral evidence, depositions, or, at the court's discretion, affidavits. If affidavits are admitted, written interrogatories may be served on the affiants, and answering affidavits may also be filed. If the applicant is indigent, counsel should petition the court to pay for investigative or expert services, where necessary to prepare the case.

At the hearing itself, subpoenas are available to compel the attendance and testimony of witnesses.

Under Rule 8(c) of the Rules Governing Section 2254 cases, the applicant has a right to counsel at the hearing. Section 2243 gives the petitioner the right to be present at the hearing, and the party to whom the petition is directed has the burden of producing the prisoner.

The rules governing discovery and evidentiary hearings for motions filed under section 2255 are slightly different from those that govern habeas corpus petitions filed under section 2254.

Rule 6(a) of the Rules Governing § 2255 Proceedings permits the movant to utilize either the discovery procedures set out in Rules 26 through 37 of the Federal Rules of Civil Procedure or in Rule 16 of the Federal Rules of Criminal Procedure. The criminal rule may be advantageous to the movant in some circumstances because of its reciprocal discovery provisions. Rule 6(a) also permits the court to appoint counsel to the movant if necessary to facilitate the discovery process.

Section 2255 provides that the court should grant a hearing unless the motion itself "conclusively show[s] that the prisoner is entitled to no relief," although the hearing contemplated is not necessarily an evidentiary hearing. Whether to grant an evidentiary hearing is governed by the standards of *Townsend v. Sain*, 372 U.S. 293, 9 L.Ed.2d 770, 83 S.Ct. 745 (1963), partially overruled by, *Keeney v. Tamayo-Reyes*, 504 U.S. 1, 118 L.Ed.2d 318, 112 S.Ct. 1715 (1992). Very generally, these cases require that a hearing be held where, through no fault of the applicant, the state court made no determination on a factual question, the state court's determination is not supported by the record, or the determination was made after an unfair procedure. In addition, where the application alleges facts that, if proved, would entitle the petitioner to relief, a hearing should also be granted. It should be noted that while 28 U.S.C.S.§ 2254(e)(2), an AEDPA addition, has curtailed the availability of evidentiary hearings in 2254 cases, where the lack of factual findings in the state court was the fault of the petitioner, there is no parallel provision governing 2255 motions.

Under Rule 8(c) of the Rules Governing § 2255 Proceedings, the court must appoint counsel for the indigent movant if it grants an evidentiary hearing. The prisoner's presence is required under section 2255 only if there are "substantial issues of fact" relating to events in which the prisoner participated." *United States v. Hayman*, 342 U.S. 205, 223 (1952)

Relief and Appeals
28 USCS § 2253

Because an applicant seeking a writ of habeas corpus is alleging that he is in custody illegally, the granting of an unconditional writ would require his immediate release. Not surprisingly, this is the remedy of last resort. Most writs are granted conditionally, directing the state either to retry or re-sentence the prisoner within a certain period of time or release him.

Appeals

As in all civil cases, the clerk of the district court must receive notice of appeal from the party seeking review of the final judgment on a habeas corpus petition under sections 2254 or 2241 or a motion under 2255 within thirty days of the entry of the judgment appealed from FRAP 4(a) and 28 USCS § 2107. An exception to this rule exists for prisoners, who need only place the notice within the prison's mail system within thirty days of the entry of the judgment appealed from. FRAP 4(c)(1). The notice must comply with FRAP 3(c)'s formal requirements for a notice of appeal. FRAP 3(c)(5) suggests that parties use the form appended to the Federal Rules of Appellate Procedure.

However, unlike other federal civil litigants, state prisoners appealing the denial of a habeas corpus petition under section 2254 and federal prisoners appealing the denial of a 2255 motion do not have an appeal as of right. Rather, under 28 USCS § 2253, the prisoner must obtain permission to appeal by seeking a certificate of appealability, commonly known as a "COA." The request for a COA must contain a "substantial showing of the denial of a constitutional right." 28 USCS § 2253(c)(2). A COA may be issued either by the district court or the court of appeals, and must specify the issue or issues that it covers, each of which meets the "substantial showing" test. The COA requirement does not apply to denials of habeas corpus petitions filed under § 2241. *Sugarman v. Pitzer*, 170 F.3d 1145 (D.C. C9ir. 1999).

An applicant should first seek a COA from the district judge. The request should be as broad as possible, since the appellate court can only entertain an appeal of issues covered by the COA. A petitioner can request a COA from the district court before filing a notice of appeal, but doing so does not toll the thirty-day period within which a notice of appeal must be filed. If the court has not ruled on the request for a COA by the time the notice of appeal is filed, FRAP 22(b)(1) requires the district court at that point to either grant a COA or explain why it is not doing so. If the district court denies the request for a COA, under FRAP 22(b)(1) it must forward the statement of denial to the court of appeals along with the notice of appeal. The petitioner then may, but is not required to, formally request that the court of appeals grant the COA. FRAP 22(b)(1)). If the petitioner does not, the court will treat the notice of appeal as a request for a COA and rule on it. FRAP 22(b)(2).

A party that does not prevail in the court of appeals has the right under FRAP 40 to seek rehearing from the panel and under FRAP 35 to seek rehearing en banc. Although § 2253 limits the issues that the court of appeals can entertain to those specified in the COA, § 2253 does not curtail the right to rehearing or rehearing *en banc*.

A petition for a writ of certiorari must be filed within ninety days of the "entry of the judgment" appealed from or, if rehearing was sought, within ninety days from the denial of rehearing. Supreme Court Rules 13.1, 13.3. 28 U.S.C.S. § 2253 does not impact on these time periods.

Second Applications
28 USCS § 2244

Once a habeas corpus petition has been disposed of on its merits, 28 USCS §§ 2244(a) and (b) strictly limit the filing of second or successive applications. The rules differ slightly depending on whether the prisoner is proceeding under section 2254 or 2255.

A claim contained in a state prisoner's successive petition that was presented in a prior petition "shall be dismissed." 28 USCS § 2244 (b)(1). However, this applies only to claims that were disposed on the merits. If a claim was dismissed without adjudication on the merits to permit the petitioner to return to exhaust an unexhausted claim, or for some other reason, then the re-filing of that claim in the district court is not considered a successive application. *Slack v. McDaniel*, 529 U.S. 473, 146 L.Ed.2d 542, 120 S.Ct. 1595 (2000).

Section 2244(b) establishes the court of appeals as the "gatekeeper" for successive applications filed by state prisoners. A prisoner who wishes to file a successive petition containing new claims must first move in the court of appeals for an order authorizing the district court to consider the petition. The court can grant permission only if it finds that the petitioner has made a prima facie showing that the new claims rely on a previously unavailable new rule of constitutional law that the Supreme Court has made retroactive to cases on collateral review, or that the applicant has satisfied a stringent cause and prejudice test. 28 USCS § 2244(b)(2). Under this test, the petitioner must show both that the factual predicate for the claim could not have been discovered previously through due diligence and that there is clear and convincing evidence that, but for the constitutional error, no reasonable fact finding would have convicted the petitioner.

If the court of appeals grants permission to file a successive petition, the district court must review the petition under those same standards. Thus, the court of appeals can only grant the petition if it is based on a new rule of constitutional law that the Supreme

Court has made retroactive to cases on collateral review, or it finds that the stringent cause and prejudice standards described above have been satisfied.

The court of appeals' decision to grant or deny a successive application is not appealable. Thus, it cannot be the subject of a rehearing petition or a writ of certiorari. 28 U.S.C.S. § 2244(a)(3)(E). Nevertheless, Supreme Court review of a successive petition may still be available because the successive petition can be filed as an original petition in the Supreme Court, under 28 USCS § 2241(a). *Felker v. Turpin,* 518 U.S. 651,135 L.Ed.2d 827, 116 S.Ct. 2333 (1996). Under § 2242, such a Supreme Court petition must contain a statement of the reasons for not making application to the district court in the district where the applicant is held. The petitioner must also show exceptional circumstances and that adequate relief cannot be obtained in any other form or from any other court. *Felker,* supra, 518 U.S. at 665, 134 L.Ed.2d at 841, 116 S.Ct. at 2341.

Section 2255 has a similar provision for filing second or successive 2255 motions. As with section 2254 petitions, the prisoner must first obtain permission from the court of appeals under the gate-keeping system set out in § 2244(b). The § 2255 gate-keeping scheme has slightly less stringent substantive requirements, however. A second or successive 2255 petition can raise either a previously raised or a new claim. In addition, the newly discovered evidence clause requires neither due diligence nor "but for" causation between the error and the petitioner's conviction.

If the 2255 motion was filed after an unsuccessful 2241 petition, it is not treated as a second or successive motion. The reverse is also true; a 2241 petition filed after an unsuccessful 2255 motion is not considered to be a successive petition.

FEDERAL HABEAS CORPUS STATUTES

■ ■ ■

Title 28, Chapter 153. Habeas Corpus
28 USCS §§ 2241-2255
Title 28, Chapter 154. Special Proceedings
28 USCS §§ 2261-2266

VI. Particular Proceedings
Chapter 153. Habeas Corpus

28 USCS § 2241 (2002) *Subtitle*

---

§ 2241. Power to grant writ *parallel*

(a) Writs of habeas corpus may be granted by the Supreme Court, any justice thereof, the district courts and any circuit judge within their respective jurisdictions. The order of a circuit judge shall be entered in the records of the district court of the district wherein the restraint complained of is had.

(b) The Supreme Court, any justice thereof, and any circuit judge may decline to entertain an application for a writ of habeas corpus and may transfer the application for hearing and determination to the district court having jurisdiction to entertain it.

(c) The writ of habeas corpus shall not extend to a prisoner unless—

(1) He is in custody under or by color of the authority of the United States or is committed for trial before some court thereof; or

(2) He is in custody for an act done or omitted in pursuance of an Act of Congress, or an order, process, judgment or decree of a court or judge of the United States; or

(3) He is in custody in violation of the Constitution or laws or treaties of the United States; or

(4) He, being a citizen of a foreign state and domiciled therein is in custody for an act done or omitted under any alleged right, title, authority, privilege, protection, or exemption claimed under the commission, order or sanction of any foreign state, or under color thereof, the validity and effect of which depend upon the law of nations; or

(5) It is necessary to bring him into court to testify or for trial.

(d) Where an application for a writ of habeas corpus is made by a person in custody under the judgment and sentence of a State court of a State which contains two or more Federal judicial districts, the application may be filed in the district court for the district wherein such person is in custody or in the district court for the district within which the State court was held which convicted and sentenced him and each of such district courts shall have concurrent jurisdiction to entertain the application. The district court for the district wherein such an application is filed in the exercise of its discretion and in furtherance of justice may transfer the application to the other district court for hearing and determination.

HISTORY (d) and body 100T BMA

(June 25, 1948, ch 646, § 1, 62 Stat. 964; May 24, 1949, ch 139, § 112, 63 Stat. 105; Sept. 19, 1966, P.L. 89-590, 80 Stat. 811.)

§ 2242. Application

Application for a writ of habeas corpus shall be in writing signed and verified by the person for whose relief it is intended or by someone acting in his behalf.

It shall allege the facts concerning the applicant's commitment or detention, the name of the person who has custody over him and by virtue of what claim or authority, if known.

It may be amended or supplemented as provided in the rules of procedure applicable to civil actions. If addressed to the Supreme Court, a justice thereof or a circuit judge it shall state the reasons for not making application to the district court of the district in which the applicant is held.

HISTORY

(June 25, 1948, ch 646, § 1, 62 Stat. 965.)

28 USCS § 2243 (2002)   Subtitle

---

§ 2243. Issuance of writ; return; hearing; decision

A court, justice or judge entertaining an application for a writ of habeas corpus shall forthwith award the writ or issue an order directing the respondent to show cause why the writ should not be granted, unless it appears from the application that the applicant or person detained is not entitled thereto.

The writ, or order to show cause shall be directed to the person having custody of the person detained. It shall be returned within three days unless for good cause additional time, not exceeding twenty days, is allowed.

The person to whom the writ or order is directed shall make a return certifying the true cause of the detention.

When the writ or order is returned a day shall be set for hearing, not more than five days after the return unless for good cause additional time is allowed.

Unless the application for the writ and the return present only issues of law the person to whom the writ is directed shall be required to produce at the hearing the body of the person detained.

The applicant or the person detained may, under oath, deny any of the facts set forth in the return or allege any other material facts.

The return and all suggestions made against it may be amended, by leave of court, before or after being filed.

The court shall summarily hear and determine the facts, and dispose of the matter as law and justice require.

HISTORY

(June 25, 1948, ch 646, § 1, 62 Stat. 965.)

§ 2244. Finality of determination

(a) No circuit or district judge shall be required to entertain an application for a writ of habeas corpus to inquire into the detention of a person pursuant to a judgment of a court of the United States if it appears that the legality of such detention has been determined by a judge or court of the United States on a prior application for a writ of habeas corpus, except as provided in section 2255.

(b) (1) A claim presented in a second or successive habeas corpus application under section 2254 that was presented in a prior application shall be dismissed.

(2) A claim presented in a second or successive habeas corpus application under section 2254 that was not presented in a prior application shall be dismissed unless—

(A) the applicant shows that the claim relies on a new rule of constitutional law, made retroactive to cases on collateral review by the Supreme Court, that was previously unavailable; or

(B) (i) the factual predicate for the claim could not have been discovered previously through the exercise of due diligence; and

(ii) the facts underlying the claim, if proven and viewed in light of the evidence as a whole, would be sufficient to establish by clear and convincing evidence that, but for constitutional error, no reasonable factfinder would have found the applicant guilty of the underlying offense.

(3) (A) Before a second or successive application permitted by this section is filed in the district court, the applicant shall move in the appropriate court of appeals for an order authorizing the district court to consider the application.

(B) A motion in the court of appeals for an order authorizing the district court to consider a second or successive application shall be determined by a three-judge panel of the court of appeals.

(C) The court of appeals may authorize the filing of a successive application only if it determines that the application makes a prima facie showing that the application satisfies the requirements of this subsection.

(D) The court of appeals shall grant or deny the authorization to file a second or successive application not later than thirty days after the filing of the motion.

(E) The grant or denial of an authorization by a court of appeals to file a second or successive application shall not be appealable and shall not be the subject of a petition for rehearing or for a writ of certiorari.

(4) A district court shall dismiss any claim presented in a second or successive application that the court of appeals has authorized to be filed unless the applicant shows that the claim satisfies the requirements of this section.

(c) In a habeas corpus proceeding brought in behalf of a person in custody pursuant to the judgment of a State court, a prior judgment of the Supreme Court of the United States on an appeal or review by a writ of certiorari at the instance of the prisoner of the decision of such State court, shall be conclusive as to all issues of fact or law with respect to an asserted denial of a Federal right which constitutes ground for discharge in a habeas corpus proceeding, actually adjudicated by the Supreme Court therein, unless the applicant for the writ of habeas corpus shall plead and the court shall find the existence of a material and controlling fact which did not appear in the record of the proceeding in the Supreme Court and the court shall further find that the applicant for the writ of habeas corpus could not have caused such fact to appear in such record by the exercise of reasonable diligence.

(d) (1) A 1-year period of limitation shall apply to an application for a writ of habeas corpus by a person in custody pursuant to the judgment of a State court. The limitation period shall run from the latest of—

(A) the date on which the judgment became final by the conclusion of direct review or the expiration of the time for seeking such review;

(B) the date on which the impediment to filing an application created by State action in violation of the Constitution or laws of the United States is removed, if the applicant was prevented from filing by such State action;

(C) the date on which the constitutional right asserted was initially recognized by the Supreme Court, if the right has been newly recognized by the Supreme Court and made retroactively applicable to cases on collateral review; or

(D) the date on which the factual predicate of the claim or claims presented could have been discovered through the exercise of due diligence.

(2) The time during which a properly filed application for State post-conviction or other collateral review with respect to the pertinent judgment or claim is pending shall not be counted toward any period of limitation under this subsection.

HISTORY

(June 25, 1948, ch 646, § 1, 62 Stat. 965; Nov. 2, 1966, P.L. 89-711, § 1, 80 Stat. 1104.)

(As amended April 24, 1996, P.L. 104-132, Title I, §§ 101, 106, 110 Stat. 1217, 1220.)

28 USCS § 2245 (2002)

§ 2245. Certificate of trial judge admissible in evidence

On the hearing of an application for a writ of habeas corpus to inquire into the legality of the detention of a person pursuant to a judgment the certificate of the judge who presided at the trial resulting in the judgment, setting forth the facts occurring at the trial, shall be admissible in evidence. Copies of the certificate shall be filed with the court in which the application is pending and in the court in which the trial took place.

HISTORY

(June 25, 1948, ch 646, § 1, 62 Stat. 966.)

28 USCS § 2246 (2002)

§ 2246. Evidence; depositions; affidavits

On application for a writ of habeas corpus, evidence may be taken orally or by deposition, or, in the discretion of the judge, by affidavit. If affidavits are admitted any party shall have the right to propound written interrogatories to the affiants, or to file answering affidavits.

HISTORY

(June 25, 1948, ch 646, § 1, 62 Stat. 966.)

28 USCS § 2247 (2002)

§ 2247. Documentary evidence

On application for a writ of habeas corpus documentary evidence, transcripts of proceedings upon arraignment, plea and sentence and a transcript of the oral testimony introduced on any previous similar application by or in behalf of the same petitioner, shall be admissible in evidence.

HISTORY

(June 25, 1948, ch 646, § 1, 62 Stat. 966.)

§ 2248. Return or answer; conclusiveness

The allegations of a return to the writ of habeas corpus or of an answer to an order to show cause in a habeas corpus proceeding, if not traversed, shall be accepted as true except to the extent that the judge finds from the evidence that they are not true.

HISTORY

(June 25, 1948, ch 646, § 1, 62 Stat. 966.)

28 USCS § 2249 (2002)

§ 2249. Certified copies of indictment, plea and judgment; duty of respondent

On application for a writ of habeas corpus to inquire into the detention of any person pursuant to a judgment of a court of the United States, the respondent shall promptly file with the court certified copies of the indictment, plea of petitioner and the judgment, or such of them as may be material to the questions raised, if the petitioner fails to attach them to his petition, and same shall be attached to the return to the writ, or to the answer to the order to show cause.

HISTORY

(June 25, 1948, ch 646, § 1, 62 Stat. 966.)

28 USCS § 2250 (2002)

§2250. Indigent petitioner entitled to documents without cost

If on any application for a writ of habeas corpus an order has been made permitting the petitioner to prosecute the application in forma pauperis, the clerk of any court of the United States shall furnish to the petitioner without cost certified copies of such documents or parts of the record on file in his office as may be required by order of the judge before whom the application is pending.

HISTORY

(June 25, 1948, ch 646, § 1, 62 Stat. 966.)

28 USCS § 2251 (2002)

§ 2251. Stay of state court proceedings

A justice or judge of the United States before whom a habeas corpus proceeding is pending, may, before final judgment or after final judgment of discharge, or pending appeal, stay any proceeding against the person detained in any State court or by or under the authority of any State for any matter involved in the habeas corpus proceeding.

After the granting of such a stay, any such proceeding in any State court or by or under the authority of any State shall be void. If no stay is granted, any such proceeding shall be as valid as if no habeas corpus proceedings or appeal were pending.

HISTORY

(June 25, 1948, ch 646, § 1, 62 Stat. 966.)

28 USCS § 2252 (2002)

§ 2252. Notice

Prior to the hearing of a habeas corpus proceeding in behalf of a person in custody of State officers or by virtue of State laws notice shall be served on the attorney general or other appropriate officer of such State as the justice or judge at the time of issuing the writ shall direct.

HISTORY

(June 25, 1948, ch 646, § 1, 62 Stat. 967.)

28 USCS § 2253 (2002)

§2253. Appeal

(a) In a habeas corpus proceeding or a proceeding under section 2255 before a district judge, the final order shall be subject to review, on appeal, by the court of appeals for the circuit in which the proceeding is held.

(b) There shall be no right of appeal from a final order in a proceeding to test the validity of a warrant to remove to another district or place for commitment or trial a person charged with a criminal offense against the United States, or to test the validity of such person's detention pending removal proceedings.

(c) (1) Unless a circuit justice or judge issues a certificate of appealability, an appeal may not be taken to the court of appeals from—

> (A) the final order in a habeas corpus proceeding in which the detention complained of arises out of process issued by a State court; or

> (B) the final order in a proceeding under section 2255.

(2) A certificate of appealability may issue under paragraph (1) only if the applicant has made a substantial showing of the denial of a constitutional right.

(3) The certificate of appealability under paragraph (1) shall indicate which specific issue or issues satisfy the showing required by paragraph (2).

HISTORY

(June 25, 1948, ch 646, § 1, 62 Stat. 967; May 24, 1949, ch 139, § 113, 63 Stat. 105; Oct. 31, 1951, ch 655, § 52, 65 Stat. 727.)

(As amended April 24, 1996, P.L. 104-132, Title I, § 102, 110 Stat. 1217.)

28 USCS § 2254 (2002)

§ 2254. State custody; remedies in Federal courts

(a) The Supreme Court, a Justice thereof, a circuit judge, or a district court shall entertain an application for a writ of habeas corpus in behalf of a person in custody pursuant to the judgment of a State court only on the ground that he is in custody in violation of the Constitution or laws or treaties of the United States.

(b) (1) An application for a writ of habeas corpus on behalf of a person in custody pursuant to the judgment of a State court shall not be granted unless it appears that—

   (A) the applicant has exhausted the remedies available in the courts of the State; or

   (B) (i) there is an absence of available State corrective process; or

      (ii) circumstances exist that render such process ineffective to protect the rights of the applicant.

(2) An application for a writ of habeas corpus may be denied on the merits, notwithstanding the failure of the applicant to exhaust the remedies available in the courts of the State.

(3) A State shall not be deemed to have waived the exhaustion requirement or be estopped from reliance upon the requirement unless the State, through counsel, expressly waives the requirement.

(c) An applicant shall not be deemed to have exhausted the remedies available in the courts of the State, within the meaning of this section, if he has the right under the law of the State to raise, by any available procedure, the question presented.

(d) An application for a writ of habeas corpus on behalf of a person in custody pursuant to the judgment of a State court shall not be granted with respect to any claim that was adjudicated on the merits in State court proceedings unless the adjudication of the claim—

(1) resulted in a decision that was contrary to, or involved an unreasonable application of, clearly established Federal law, as determined by the Supreme Court of the United States; or

(2) resulted in a decision that was based on an unreasonable determination of the facts in light of the evidence presented in the State court proceeding.

(e) (1) In a proceeding instituted by an application for a writ of habeas corpus by a person in custody pursuant to the judgment of a State court, a determination of a factual issue made by a State court shall be presumed to be correct. The applicant shall have the burden of rebutting the presumption of correctness by clear and convincing evidence.

(2) If the applicant has failed to develop the factual basis of a claim in State court proceedings, the court shall not hold an evidentiary hearing on the claim unless the applicant shows that—

(A) the claim relies on—

(i) a new rule of constitutional law, made retroactive to cases on collateral review by the Supreme Court, that was previously unavailable; or

(ii) a factual predicate that could not have been previously discovered through the exercise of due diligence; and

(B) the facts underlying the claim would be sufficient to establish by clear and convincing evidence that but for constitutional error, no reasonable factfinder would have found the applicant guilty of the underlying offense.

(f) If the applicant challenges the sufficiency of the evidence adduced in such State court proceeding to support the State court's determination of a factual issue made therein, the applicant, if able, shall produce that part of the record pertinent to a determination of the sufficiency of the evidence to support such determination. If the applicant, because of indigency or other reason is unable to produce such part of the record, then the State shall produce such part of the record and the Federal court shall direct the State to do so by order directed to an appropriate State official. If the State cannot provide such pertinent part of the record, then the court shall determine under the existing facts and circumstances what weight shall be given to the State court's factual determination.

(g) A copy of the official records of the State court, duly certified by the clerk of such court to be a true and correct copy of a finding, judicial opinion, or other reliable written indicia showing such a factual determination by the State court shall be admissible in the Federal court proceeding.

(h) Except as provided in section 408 of the Controlled Substance Acts [21 USCS §848], in all proceedings brought under this section, and any subsequent proceedings on review, the court may appoint counsel for an applicant who is or becomes financially unable to afford counsel, except as provided by a rule promulgated by the Supreme Court pursuant to statutory authority. Appointment of counsel under this section shall be governed by section 3006A of title 18.

(i) The ineffectiveness or incompetence of counsel during Federal or State collateral post-conviction proceedings shall not be a ground for relief in a proceeding arising under section 2254.

HISTORY

(June 25, 1948, ch 646, § 1, 62 Stat. 967; Nov. 2, 1966, P.L. 89-711, § 2, 80 Stat. 1105.)

(As amended April 24, 1996, P.L. 104-132, Title I, § 104, 110 Stat. 1218.)

HISTORY; ANCILLARY LAWS, AND DIRECTIVES

Prior law and revision:

This section is declaratory of existing law as affirmed by the Supreme Court. (See Ex parte Hawk (1944) 321 US 114, 88 L Ed 572, 64 S Ct 448.) This section was enacted as amended by the Senate with the following explanation:

"This amendment is proposed by the Judicial Conference of Senior Circuit Judges.

"It has three purposes. The first is to eliminate from the prohibition of the section applications in behalf of prisoners in custody under authority of a State officer but whose custody has not been directed by the judgment of a State court. If the section were applied to applications by persons detained solely under authority of a State officer it would unduly hamper Federal courts in the protection of Federal officers prosecuted for acts committed in the course of official duty.

"The second purpose is to eliminate, as a ground of Federal jurisdiction to review by habeas corpus judgments of State courts, the proposition that the State court has denied a prisoner a 'fair adjudication of the legality of his detention under the Constitution and laws of the United States.' The Judicial Conference believes that this would be an undesirable ground for Federal jurisdiction in addition to exhaustion of State remedies or lack of adequate remedy in the State courts because it would permit proceedings in the Federal court on this ground before the petitioner had exhausted his State remedies. This ground would, of course, always be open to a petitioner to assert in the Federal court after he had exhausted his State remedies or if he had no adequate State remedy.

"The third purpose is to substitute detailed and specific language for the phrase 'no adequate remedy available.' That phrase is not sufficiently specific and precise, and its meaning should, therefore be spelled out in more detail in the section as is done by the amendment."

Amendments:

1966. Act Nov. 2, 1966, in the section heading, substituted "Federal" for "State"; added subsec. (a); designated existing matter as subsecs. (b) and (c); and added subsecs. (d)-(f).

1996. Act April 24, 1996 substituted subsec. (b) for one which read: "(b) An application for a writ of habeas corpus in behalf of a person in custody pursuant to the judgment of a State court shall not be granted unless it appears that the applicant has exhausted the remedies available in the courts of the State, or that there is either an absence of available State corrective process or the existence of circumstances rendering such process ineffective to protect the rights of the prisoner."; redesignated subsecs. (d)-(f) as subsecs. (e)-(g), respectively; added subsec. (d); substituted subsec. (e) for one which read:

"(e) In any proceeding instituted in a Federal court by an application for a writ of habeas corpus by a person in custody pursuant to the judgment of a State court, a determination after a hearing on the merits of a factual issue, made by a State court of competent jurisdiction in a proceeding to which the applicant for the writ and the State or an officer or agent thereof were parties, evidenced by a written finding, written opinion, or other reliable and adequate written indicia, shall be presumed to be correct, unless the applicant shall establish or it shall otherwise appear, or the respondent shall admit—

"(1) that the merits of the factual dispute were not resolved in the State court hearing;

"(2) that the fact finding procedure employed by the State court was not adequate to afford a full and fair hearing;

"(3) that the material facts were not adequately developed at the State court hearing;

"(4) that the State court lacked jurisdiction of the subject matter or over the person of the applicant in the State court proceeding;

"(5) that the applicant was an indigent and the State court, in deprivation of his constitutional right, failed to appoint counsel to represent him in the State court proceeding;

"(6) that the applicant did not receive a full, fair, and adequate hearing in the State court proceeding; or

"(7) that the applicant was otherwise denied due process of law in the State court proceeding;

"(8) or unless that part of the record of the State court proceeding in which the determination of such factual issue was made, pertinent to a determination of the sufficiency of the evidence to support such factual determination, is produced as provided for hereinafter, and the Federal court on a consideration of such part of the record as a whole concludes that such factual determination is not fairly supported by the record:

"And in an evidentiary hearing in the proceeding in the Federal court, when due proof of such factual determination has been made, unless the existence of one or more of the circumstances respectively set forth in paragraphs numbered (1) to (7), inclusive, is shown by the applicant, otherwise appears, or is admitted by the respondent, or unless the court concludes pursuant to the provisions of paragraph numbered (8) that the record in the State court proceeding, considered as a whole, does not fairly support such factual determination, the burden shall rest upon the applicant to establish by convincing evidence that the factual determination by the State court was erroneous."; and added subsecs. (h) and (i).

§ 2255. Federal custody; remedies on motion attacking sentence

A prisoner in custody under sentence of a court established by Act of Congress claiming the right to be released upon the ground that the sentence was imposed in violation of the Constitution or laws of the United States, or that the court was without jurisdiction to impose such sentence, or that the sentence was in excess of the maximum authorized by law, or is otherwise subject to collateral attack, may move the court which imposed the sentence to vacate, set aside or correct the sentence.

Unless the motion and the files and records of the case conclusively show that the prisoner is entitled to no relief, the court shall cause notice thereof to be served upon the United States attorney, grant a prompt hearing thereon, determine the issues and make findings of fact and conclusions of law with respect thereto. If the court finds that the judgment was rendered without jurisdiction, or that the sentence imposed was not authorized by law or otherwise open to collateral attack, or that there has been such a denial or infringement of the constitutional rights of the prisoner as to render the judgment vulnerable to collateral attack, the court shall vacate and set the judgment aside and shall discharge the prisoner or resentence him or grant a new trial or correct the sentence as may appear appropriate.

A court may entertain and determine such motion without requiring the production of the prisoner at the hearing.

An appeal may be taken to the court of appeals from the order entered on the motion as from the final judgment on application for a writ of habeas corpus.

An application for a writ of habeas corpus in behalf of a prisoner who is authorized to apply for relief by motion pursuant to this section, shall not be entertained if it appears that the applicant has failed to apply for relief, by motion, to the court which sentenced him, or that such court has denied him relief, unless it also appears that the remedy by motion is inadequate or ineffective to test the legality of his detention.

A 1-year period of limitation shall apply to a motion under this section. The limitation period shall run from the latest of

(1) the date on which the judgment of conviction becomes final;

(2) the date on which the impediment to making a motion created by governmental action in violation of the Constitution or laws of the United States is removed, if the movant was prevented from making a motion by such governmental action;

(3) the date on which the right asserted was initially recognized by the Supreme Court, if that right has been newly recognized by the Supreme Court and made retroactively applicable to cases on collateral review; or

(4) the date on which the facts supporting the claim or claims presented could have been discovered through the exercise of due diligence.

Except as provided in section 408 of the Controlled Substances Act [21 USCS § 848], in all proceedings brought under this section, and any subsequent proceedings on review, the court may appoint counsel, except as provided by a rule promulgated by the Supreme Court pursuant to statutory authority. Appointment of counsel under this section shall be governed by section 3006A of title 18. A second or successive motion must be certified as provided in section 2244 by a panel of the appropriate court of appeals to contain—

(1) newly discovered evidence that, if proven and viewed in light of the evidence as a whole, would be sufficient to establish by clear and convincing evidence that no reasonable factfinder would have found the movant guilty of the offense; or

(2) a new rule of constitutional law, made retroactive to cases on collateral review by the Supreme Court, that was previously unavailable.

HISTORY

(June 25, 1948, ch 646, § 1, 62 Stat. 967; May 24, 1949, ch 139, § 114, 63 Stat. 105.)

(As amended April 24, 1996, P.L. 104-132, Title I, § 105, 110 Stat. 1220.)

Part VI. Particular Proceedings
Title
Chapter 154.
Special Habeas Corpus Procedures in Capital Cases

28 USCS § 2261 (2002)   *Subtitle*

---

§ 2261. Prisoners in state custody subject to capital sentence; appointment of counsel; requirement of rule of court or statute; procedures for appointment

(a) This chapter [28 USCS §§ 2261 et seq.] shall apply to cases arising under section 2254 brought by prisoners in State custody who are subject to a capital sentence. It shall apply only if the provisions of subsections (b) and (c) are satisfied.

(b) This chapter [28 USCS §§ 2261 et seq.] is applicable if a State establishes by statute, rule of its court of last resort, or by another agency authorized by State law, a mechanism for the appointment, compensation, and payment of reasonable litigation expenses of competent counsel in State post-conviction proceedings brought by indigent prisoners whose capital convictions and sentences have been upheld on direct appeal to the court of last resort in the State or have otherwise become final for State law purposes. The rule of court or statute must provide standards of competency for the appointment of such counsel.

(c) Any mechanism for the appointment, compensation, and reimbursement of counsel as provided in subsection (b) must offer counsel to all State prisoners under capital sentence and must provide for the entry of an order by a court of record—

(1) appointing one or more counsels to represent the prisoner upon a finding that the prisoner is indigent and accepted the offer or is unable competently to decide whether to accept or reject the offer;

(2) finding, after a hearing if necessary, that the prisoner rejected the offer of counsel and made the decision with an understanding of its legal consequences; or

(3) denying the appointment of counsel upon a finding that the prisoner is not indigent.

(d) No counsel appointed pursuant to subsections (b) and (c) to represent a State prisoner under capital sentence shall have previously represented the prisoner at trial or on direct appeal in the case for which the appointment is made unless the prisoner and counsel expressly request continued representation.

(e) The ineffectiveness or incompetence of counsel during State or Federal post-conviction proceedings in a capital case shall not be a ground for relief in a proceeding arising under section 2254. This limitation shall not preclude the appointment of different counsel, on the court's own motion or at the request of the prisoner, at any phase of State or Federal post-conviction proceedings on the basis of the ineffectiveness or incompetence of counsel in such proceedings.

HISTORY

(Added April 24, 1996, P.L. 104-132, Title I, § 107(a), 110 Stat. 1221.)

28 USCS § 2262 (2002)   Subtitle

---

§ 2262. Mandatory stay of execution; duration; limits on stays of execution; successive petitions

(a) Upon the entry in the appropriate State court of record of an order under section 2261(c), a warrant or order setting an execution date for a State prisoner shall be stayed upon application to any court that would have jurisdiction over any proceedings filed under section 2254. The application shall recite that the State has invoked the post-conviction review procedures of this chapter [28 USCS §§ 2261 et seq.] and that the scheduled execution is subject to stay.

(b) A stay of execution granted pursuant to subsection (a) shall expire if—

(1) a State prisoner fails to file a habeas corpus application under section 2254 within the time required in section 2263;

(2) before a court of competent jurisdiction, in the presence of counsel, unless the prisoner has competently and knowingly waived such counsel, and after having been advised of the consequences, a State prisoner under capital sentence waives the right to pursue habeas corpus review under section 2254; or

(3) a State prisoner files a habeas corpus petition under section 2254 within the time required by section 2263 and fails to make a substantial showing of the denial of a Federal right or is denied relief in the district court or at any subsequent stage of review.

(c) If one of the conditions in subsection (b) has occurred, no Federal court thereafter shall have the authority to enter a stay of execution in the case, unless the court of appeals approves the filing of a second or successive application under section 2244(b).

HISTORY

(Added April 24, 1996, P.L. 104-132, Title I, § 107(a), 110 Stat. 1222.)

28 USCS § 2263 (2002)   *subtitle*

§ 2263. Filing of habeas corpus application; time requirements; tolling rules

(a) Any application under this chapter [28 USCS §§ 2261 et seq.] for habeas corpus relief under section 2254 must be filed in the appropriate district court not later than 180 days after final State court affirmance of the conviction and sentence on direct review or the expiration of the time for seeking such review.

(b) The time requirements established by subsection (a) shall be tolled—

(1) from the date that a petition for certiorari is filed in the Supreme Court until the date of final disposition of the

petition if a State prisoner files the petition to secure review by the Supreme Court of the affirmance of a capital sentence on direct review by the court of last resort of the State or other final State court decision on direct review;

(2) from the date on which the first petition for post-conviction review or other collateral relief is filed until the final State court disposition of such petition; and

(3) during an additional period not to exceed thirty days, if—

(A) a motion for an extension of time is filed in the Federal district court that would have jurisdiction over the case upon the filing of a habeas corpus application under section 2254; and

(B) a showing of good cause is made for the failure to file the habeas corpus application within the time period established by this section.

HISTORY

(Added April 24, 1996, P.L. 104-132, Title I, § 107(a), 110 Stat. 1223.)

28 USCS § 2264 (2002)

§ 2264. Scope of federal review; district court adjudications

(a) Whenever a State prisoner under capital sentence files a petition for habeas corpus relief to which this chapter [28 USCS §§ 2261 et seq.] applies, the district court shall only consider a claim or claims that have been raised and decided on the merits in the State courts, unless the failure to raise the claim properly is—

(1) the result of State action in violation of the Constitution or laws of the United States;

(2) the result of the Supreme Court's recognition of a new Federal right that is made retroactively applicable; or

(3) based on a factual predicate that could not have been discovered through the exercise of due diligence in time to present the claim for State or Federal post-conviction review.

(b) Following review subject to subsections (a), (d), and (e) of section 2254, the court shall rule on the claims properly before it.

HISTORY

(Added April 24, 1996, P.L. 104-132, Title I, § 107(a), 110 Stat. 1223.)

28 USCS § 2265 (2002)

§ 2265. Application to state unitary review procedure

(a) For purposes of this section, a "unitary review" procedure means a State procedure that authorizes a person under sentence of death to raise, in the course of direct review of the judgment, such claims as could be raised on collateral attack. This chapter [28 USCS §§ 2261 et seq.] shall apply, as provided in this section, in relation to a State unitary review procedure if the State establishes by rule of its court of last resort or by statute a mechanism for the appointment, compensation, and payment of reasonable litigation expenses of competent counsel in the unitary review proceedings, including expenses relating to the litigation of collateral claims in the proceedings. The rule of court or statute must provide standards of competency for the appointment of such counsel.

(b) To qualify under this section, a unitary review procedure must include an offer of counsel following trial for the purpose of representation on unitary review, and entry of an order, as provided in section 2261(c), concerning appointment of counsel or waiver or denial of appointment of counsel for that purpose. No counsel appointed to represent the prisoner in the unitary review proceedings shall have previously represented the prisoner at trial in the case for which the appointment is made unless the prisoner and counsel expressly request continued representation.

(c) Sections 2262, 2263, 2264, and 2266 shall apply in relation to cases involving a sentence of death from any State having a unitary review procedure that qualifies under this section. References to State "post-conviction review" and "direct review" in such sections shall be understood as referring to unitary review under the State procedure. The reference in section 2262(a) to "an order under section 2261(c)" shall be understood as referring to the post-trial order under subsection (b) concerning representation in the unitary review proceedings, but if a transcript of the trial proceedings is unavailable at the time of the filing of such an order in the appropriate State court, then the start of the 180-day limitation period under section 2263 shall be deferred until a transcript is made available to the prisoner or counsel of the prisoner.

HISTORY

(Added April 24, 1996, P.L. 104-132, Title I, § 107(a), 110 Stat. 1223.)

28 USCS § 2266 (2002)

§ 2266. Limitation periods for determining applications and motions

(a) The adjudication of any application under section 2254 that is subject to this chapter [28 USCS §§ 2261 et seq.], and the adjudication of any motion under section 2255 by a person under sentence of death, shall be given priority by the district court and by the court of appeals over all noncapital matters.

(b) (1) (A) A district court shall render a final determination and enter a final judgment on any application for a writ of habeas corpus brought under this chapter [28 USCS §§ 2261 et seq.] in a capital case not later than 180 days after the date on which the application is filed.

(B) A district court shall afford the parties at least 120 days in which to complete all actions, including the preparation of all pleadings and briefs, and if necessary, a hearing, prior to the submission of the case for decision.

(C) (i) A district court may delay for not more than one additional thirty-day period beyond the period specified in subparagraph (A), the rendering of a determination of an application for a writ of habeas corpus if the court issues a written order making a finding, and stating the reasons for the finding, that the ends of justice that would be served by allowing the delay outweigh the best interests of the public and the applicant in a speedy disposition of the application.

(ii) The factors, among others, that a court shall consider in determining whether a delay in the disposition of an application is warranted are as follows:

(I) Whether the failure to allow the delay would be likely to result in a miscarriage of justice.

(II) Whether the case is so unusual or so complex, due to the number of defendants, the nature of the prosecution, or the existence of novel questions of fact or law, that it is unreasonable to expect adequate briefing within the time limitations established by subparagraph (A).

(III) Whether the failure to allow a delay in a case that, taken as a whole, is not so unusual or so complex as described in subclause (II), but would otherwise deny the applicant reasonable time to obtain counsel, would unreasonably deny the applicant or the government continuity of counsel, or would deny counsel for the applicant or the government the reasonable time necessary for effective preparation, taking into account the exercise of due diligence.

(iii) No delay in disposition shall be permissible because of general congestion of the court's calendar.

(iv) The court shall transmit a copy of any order issued under clause (i) to the Director of the administrative Office of the United States Courts for inclusion in the report under paragraph (5).

(2) The time mitations under paragraph (1) shall apply to—

(A) an initial application for a writ of habeas corpus;

(B) any second or successive application for a writ of habeas corpus; and

(C) any redetermination of an application for a writ of habeas corpus following a remand by the court of appeals or the Supreme Court for further proceedings, in which case the limitation period shall run from the date the remand is ordered.

(3) (A) The time limitations under this section shall not be construed to entitle an applicant to a stay of execution, to which the applicant would otherwise not be entitled, for the purpose of litigating any application or appeal.

(B) No amendment to an application for a writ of habeas corpus under this chapter [28 USCS §§ 2261 et seq.] shall be permitted after the filing of the answer to the application, except on the grounds specified in section 2244(b).

(4) (A) The failure of a court to meet or comply with a time limitation under this section shall not be a ground for granting relief from a judgment of conviction or sentence.

(B) The State may enforce a time limitation under this section by petitioning for a writ of mandamus to the court of appeals. The court of appeals shall act on the petition for a writ of mandamus not later than thirty days after the filing of the petition.

(5) (A) The Administrative Office of the United States Courts shall submit to Congress an annual report on the compliance by the district courts with the time limitations under this section.

(B) The report described in subparagraph (A) shall include copies of the orders submitted by the district courts under paragraph (1)(B)(iv).

(c) (1) (A) A court of appeals shall hear and render a final determination of any appeal of an order granting or denying, in whole or in part, an application brought under this chapter [28 USCS §§ 2261 et seq.] in a capital case not later than 120 days after the date on which the reply brief is filed, or if no reply brief is filed, not later than 120 days after the date on which the answering brief is filed.

(B) (i) A court of appeals shall decide whether to grant a petition for rehearing or other request for rehearing en banc not later than thirty days after the date on which the petition for rehearing is filed unless a responsive pleading is required, in which case the court shall decide whether to grant the petition not later than thirty days after the date on which the responsive pleading is filed.

(ii) If a petition for rehearing or rehearing en banc is granted, the court of appeals shall hear and render a final determination of the appeal not later than 120 days after the date on which the order granting rehearing or rehearing en banc is entered.

(2) The time limitations under paragraph (1) shall apply to—

(A) an initial application for a writ of habeas corpus;

(B) any second or successive application for a writ of habeas corpus; and

(C) any redetermination of an application for a writ of habeas corpus or related appeal following a remand by the court of appeals en banc or the Supreme Court for further proceedings, in which case the limitation period shall run from the date the remand is ordered.

(3) The time limitations under this section shall not be construed to entitle an applicant to a stay of execution, to which the applicant would otherwise not be entitled, for the purpose of litigating any application or appeal.

(4) (A) The failure of a court to meet or comply with a time limitation under this section shall not be a ground for granting relief from a judgment of conviction or sentence.

(B) The State may enforce a time limitation under this section by applying for a writ of mandamus to the Supreme Court.

(5) The Administrative Office of the United States Courts shall submit to Congress an annual report on the compliance by the courts of appeals with the time limitations under this section.

HISTORY

(Added April 24, 1996, P.L. 104-132, Title I, § 107(a), 110 Stat. 1224.)

NITA

National Institute for Trial Advocacy
Notre Dame Law School
Notre Dame, Indiana 46556
(800) 225-6482 Fax (574) 271-8375
nita.1@nd.edu www.nita.org
FBA0804

9 781556 818042